Nature
Printing

Nature Printing
The Ogden Nature Center

Sterling Publishing Co., Inc., New York
A Sterling/Chapelle Book

Chapelle, Ltd.

Jo Packham
Sara Toliver
Cindy Stoeckl

Editor: Kelly Ashkettle
Art Director: Karla Haberstich
Copy Editor: Marilyn Goff
Photography: Kevin Dilley for Hazen Imaging
Photo Stylist: Suzy Skadburg
Staff: Areta Bingham, Donna Chambers,
Emily Frandsen, Lana Hall, Mackenzie Johnson,
Susan Jorgensen, Jennifer Luman,
Melissa Maynard, Barbara Milburn, Lecia Monsen,
Kim Taylor, Desirée Wybrow

Library of Congress Cataloging-in-Publication
Data Available

10 9 8 7 6 5 4 3 2 1

Published by Sterling Publishing Co., Inc.
387 Park Avenue South, New York, NY 10016
©2004 by The Ogden Nature Center
Distributed in Canada by Sterling Publishing
c/o Canadian Manda Group,
One Atlantic Avenue, Suite 105
Toronto, Ontario, Canada M6K 3E7
Distributed in Great Britain by Chrysalis Books
64 Brewery Road, London N7 9NT, England
Distributed in Australia by
Capricorn Link (Australia) Pty. Ltd.
P.O. Box 704, Windsor, NSW 2756, Australia
Printed in China
All Rights Reserved

Sterling ISBN
1-4027-0724-X

Write Us

If you have any questions or comments, please contact:

Chapelle, Ltd., Inc.,
P.O. Box 9252, Ogden, UT 84409
(801) 621-2777 • (801) 621-2788 Fax
e-mail: chapelle@chapelleltd.com
web site: chapelleltd.com

Foreword
Kabi Cook

Art takes nature as its model. — *Aristotle*

All art is but imitation of nature. — *Seneca*

Nature inspires the soul. Beauty and tranquility are found along the seashore, throughout dense forests, across vast deserts, and among mountaintops. It is in nature that one unites with the earth in a realm where clarity and creativity are enhanced. It is the beauty of nature that has inspired the creations found within these pages. Take a few moments to connect with the natural world around you. Experiment with the materials you collect and embark on nature printing and crafting adventures of your own. Experience the beauty of nature.

Table of Contents

Introduction

Nature printing is a tradition that spans centuries, with professional and amateur artists alike revealing the beauty of the natural world upon a variety of surfaces. Many cultures have deep-rooted customs of experimenting with natural elements as both an art form and a way to learn about their surroundings. Nature printing continues today as both expression and exploration for people of all ages and backgrounds.

This form of nature exploration is often used as an educational tool. Teacher/naturalists at the Ogden Nature Center and other environmental facilities around the world use nature printing techniques such as basic direct printing, rubbing, and solar printing to help children discover the natural world around them. Programs designed around tracks or animal prints that nature leaves us during snowy or rainy seasons are also used to promote nature education. There are many ways to learn from our natural environment.

There have been several methods of nature printing discovered over time. The techniques featured in this book include direct printing, gyotaku (fish rubbing), imprinting, and hammered printing. Various mediums are used and others have been suggested on a project-by-project basis. Creativity is the key. Keep in mind that nearly anything found in nature can produce a print. The following are brief descriptions of these different techniques. Step-by-step instructions are illustrated and outlined with each individual project.

Direct printing is a great method to use when beginning your nature-printing adventures. The technique consists of taking a water-based ink or a textile paint, applying it to natural materials, and pressing it directly to the chosen surface. We applied this method on several projects, creating leaf, fruit, vegetable, and floral prints on paper, various fabrics, pottery, and glassware.

Additional materials needed for direct printing include a palette, palette knife, newspaper, newsprint paper, paintbrushes or sponges, paper towels, and soft rubber brayers.

Gyotaku, or fish rubbing, is a technique that originates from Japan and is enjoyed by children and adults alike. Using water-based ink or textile paints, fish can be coated as creatively as you wish before images are transferred to your chosen medium. What distinguishes gyotaku from direct printing is the manner in which the print is created: rubbing versus pressing. Straight pins and squares of cardboard or balls of modeling clay are used to stabilize the fish while printing.

Imprinting, or creating impressions, is another nature printing technique. Pressing items found in nature into materials such as clay or cement leaves a distinct print that shows the delicate intricacies of the natural world. Imprinting requires a steady hand and attention to detail. Remnants of natural materials can sometimes become lodged in the patterns and need to be carefully removed to prevent decay. Tools often used in material removal are paintbrushes, T-pins, and tweezers.

A hard surface is needed for hammered prints. Fresh flowers are the most popular material for hammered printing. To create the smashed flower prints in this book, we placed the flowers, secured them with tape, covered them with newsprint or waxed paper, and smashed them with a hammer.

Nature has been a source of inspiration throughout the ages for artists, musicians, scientists, and laymen. Driven by the beauty of their surroundings, humans long to understand the majesty of Mother Earth. The projects in this book represent our efforts to express the wonder we feel when exploring our natural world. We hope that you, too, will take pleasure in learning from nature as you design projects of your own.

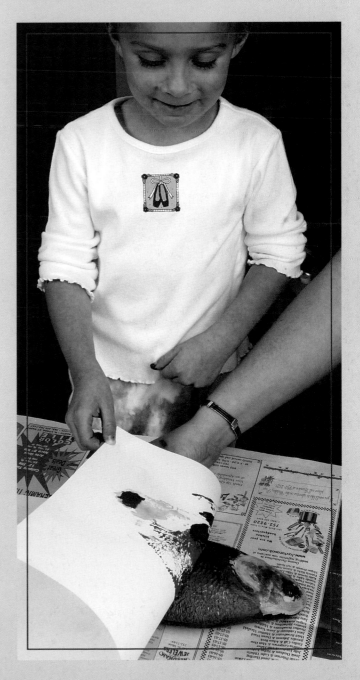

Ethics of Collecting from Nature
Rules to Follow

Collecting items from nature may seem quite harmless; however, removing plants or seeds, taking cuttings, or collecting feathers, rocks, or even dirt can negatively impact the environment and might be in violation of the law. Plants and animals live in a delicate balance with the earth, and any disturbance to them might cause serious problems.

The following are some basic rules to follow from Washington State University should you decide to collect items from nature.

• Consider the environmental impact before collecting any plant materials or other natural objects. Tufts of animal hair found on a branch might be valuable to a bird who is building a nest.

• Do not collect more than you need or will actually use. Take care of what is collected so that it is not wasted, and share extras with others.

• When collecting seeds or cuttings of plants, do not collect more than five percent or $\frac{1}{20}$ of any plant or seed of that species. Make certain you leave enough that the plant can regenerate itself and so that the wildlife that depends on the seeds or plant will not be harmed.

- Only collect whole plants from areas where indigenous vegetation will be destroyed, such as from construction sites.

- Do not collect plants, seeds, or cuttings of rare or endangered species unless they are in danger of being destroyed. Even then, contact the appropriate agencies and organizations before collecting any part of the plant.

- Avoid frequent visits to the same site, and do not encourage others to collect from the same area. Avoid damaging a site that you are visiting.

- If you find an unusual plant or one that is not familiar, assume that it is rare and do not collect cuttings or seeds from it until you find out that it is not rare.

- Respect private property. Always ask for the land owner's permission to collect on their property or to walk on their land.

- Before collecting on public land, be certain to obtain the necessary permits. It is against the law to collect items from nature in National Parks. Rocks, feathers, leaves, flowers, animal bones are all to be left where they are found, unless you have the necessary permits. Check the laws and ordinances for state and other public lands.

- Do not collect from environmentally sensitive areas such as wetlands.

- Tread lightly and do not leave an impact on the land where you have been collecting.

Spring
projects

Smashed Flowers Tote

Linda Weiskopf

Materials:

cardboard or newspaper

cutting board or wide piece of wood

dishpan or plastic storage container

flathead hammer

fresh flowers or leaves (these cannot be dry)

iron and ironing board

½ cup of salt

tote bag, T-shirt, or other fabric item such as a visor, hat, or shorts

transparent tape or wide packing tape

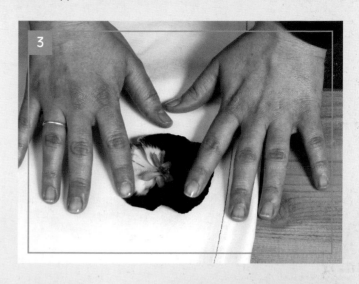

Process:

1. Wash, dry, and press tote, following manufacturer's instructions.

2. Lay tote over cutting board. *Note: If printing onto a two-layered item, make certain to place cardboard or newspaper in between each layer of fabric so print does not bleed through.*

3. Position flower on tote and cover entirely with tape to secure placement.

4. Hammer flower, paying close attention to outer edges, until you see print appear when you lift up one corner of flower (approximately one minute).

5. Carefully remove tape and lift flower from tote. Repeat as desired.

6. Mix salt with 2 gallons of water in dishpan and soak tote for 10 minutes to set color.

7. Rinse thoroughly and dry, either outdoors or in dryer.

Tips:

• You can use flowers more than once if they remain intact when removing.

• You can also smash flowers onto heavy cardstock to make personalized gift cards.

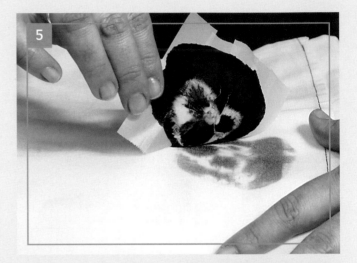

Tip: Some partial prints and lighter images give a look of dimension to the design. These can be created by using a lighter touch and not hammering the entire image.

Canvas Place Mat
Karen Stayer

Materials:

12" x 16" primed canvas

acrylic paints in desired colors

clear satin acrylic varnish

leaves

paintbrushes

paper plate

pencil

ruler

waxed paper

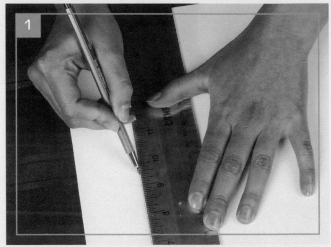

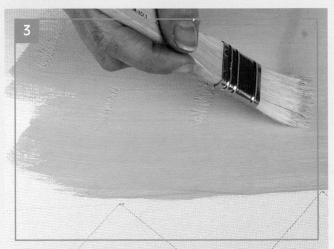

Process:

1. Using a ruler, pencil, and eraser (if needed), mark 2" border around canvas.

2. Draw desired border pattern or leave blank.

3. Paint center rectangle in selected color.

4. Paint border in selected colors. Let air-dry for one hour.

5. Place leaves on waxed paper and coat one side with paint.

6. Place leaf paint-side-down on canvas. Cover with waxed paper and gently press, then remove waxed paper and leaf.

7. Repeat as desired, and let air-dry for one hour or until dry.

8. Apply 2–3 thin coats of acrylic varnish. Let air-dry at least two hours.

Idea: *For a wonderful addition to your Thanksgiving table, try making place mats using autumn leaves and painting with vibrant reds, oranges, browns, and yellows.*

Onionskin-dyed Eggs
Yaeko Bryner

Materials:

¼ cup vinegar

cheesecloth or nylon stocking

edible leaves or herbs

fresh eggs

onionskins, beets, or red cabbage

saucepan

scissors

soft cloth

twist tie or raffia

Process:

1. Cut one 8" square from cheesecloth for each egg.

2. Wet egg with warm water.

3. Place leaf on egg in desired position.

4. Wrap egg in cheesecloth and secure tightly with twist tie.

5. Repeat for each egg.

6. Place wrapped eggs and onionskins in saucepan.

7. Fill saucepan with water and vinegar, making certain that eggs are submerged.

8. Boil eggs for approximately 10–15 minutes, until eggs are desired color.

9. Let eggs cool.

10. Unwrap eggs.

11. Remove leaf.

12. Using soft cloth and water, wipe eggs.

Tips:

- The color varies depending on how many skins you use.

- Using different skins produces different colors and shades:
    - Onionskins produce yellow and brown colors
    - Beets produce a red color (beet tops will produce a lighter pink color)
    - Red cabbage produces purple and blue colors

- For a natural shine, rub finished eggs with vegetable oil.

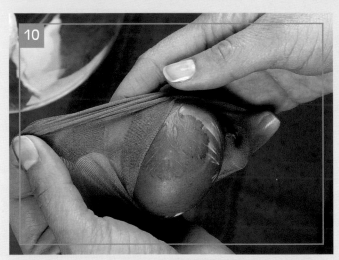

Stepping Stones
Mary McKinley and Linda Weiskopf

Materials:

3 stepping-stone molds or disposable aluminum baking pans with 11" diameters

10 pounds quick-setting cement (makes 3 stones)

acrylic paint (optional, if you want to paint the surface of the stepping stone)

bucket

cement sealer (optional)

color additive (optional, if colored cement is desired)

hand shovel or trowel

heavy plastic sheet or heavy-duty garbage bag

large thick leaves with prominent veins from plants such as rhubarb, hosta, dock, or squash; or sturdy flowers such as gerbera daisies

measuring cup

rubber gloves

sponge

stiff-bristled paintbrush

wooden craft stick

Process:

1. Pour two cups water into bucket, then slowly add bag of quick-setting cement.

2. Mix with shovel to consistency of cookie dough. Add more water, up to one cup, as needed. Add colored additive if desired.

3. Pour cement into molds, pressing and patting into place. If crumbly, put back in bucket and add ¼–½ cup of water; repour.

4. Let cement sit for one hour, using sponge to remove water as it rises to top of cement. Occasionally tap side of molds to remove any air bubbles.

5. Press leaves into cement. With craft stick, outline edge of leaves.

6. Cover cement and leaves with plastic and allow to dry slowly. *Note: Drying can take 24 hours or more.* Do not move or disturb stepping stone while drying.

7. Remove plastic. Let leaves stay in cement to slowly decompose on their own, or peel off, using paintbrush to gently remove any debris. Allow stone to dry thoroughly.

8. Remove stepping stones from molds. If desired, lightly brush paint across stones and gently wipe off with a wet sponge.

9. Apply cement sealer, following manufacturer's instructions.

Idea: *Make several stones at a time using various shapes and sizes. Place them randomly throughout your garden for a beautiful yet functional display.*

Fern-printed Rug

Suzy Skadburg

Materials:

blank stencil sheet
craft knife
cutting mat
fern fronds
masking tape
pencil
scissors
sisal rug
stencil brush

stencil paints
tape measure

Process:

1. Cut 1–2 nicely shaped sprigs from fronds.

2. Place sprig on blank stencil sheet. Using pencil, trace around each leaf.

3. Place stencil sheet on cutting mat. Using craft knife, cut out stencil.

4. Position stencil on rug and tape stencil in place. *Note: For symmetrical design, use tape measure and pencil to mark center point and even spacing.*

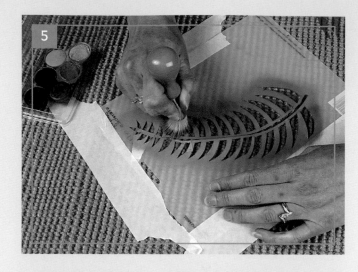

5. Dab stencil brush into desired color of paint. Using circular motion, rub paint into cutout of stencil until completely filled in, dabbing brush into paint as necessary. Let dry thoroughly.

6. Peel off stencil. Place your rug in a low traffic area for maximum durability.

Tips:

- Do not use too much paint. Rub the brush on a scrap piece of fabric to test how paint will apply.

- Periodically check the front of stencil to ensure no paint is seeping under the edges. If this happens, simply wipe off front of stencil with a paper towel.

Idea: *Stenciling is a great way to create wall borders. Here, both leaf stencils and prints were used to create this colorful design.*

Bleach-printed Pillowcase
Kabi Cook

Materials:

bleach

bucket or large pot

daisies or other flowers

flattened cardboard box

rubber gloves

newspaper

solid-colored 100% cotton pillowcase

spray bottle

4. Position flowers in desired pattern on pillowcase. *Note: These how-to photos show an allover pattern, or choose a border design like the one in the photo on page 33.*

5. Wearing gloves, fill spray bottle with bleach.

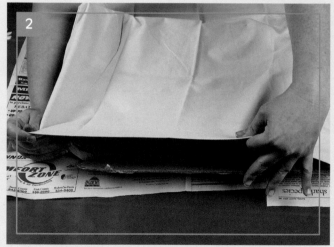

Process:

1. Spread newspaper over hard work surface. Place pillowcase on newspaper.

2. Place flattened box inside pillowcase between fabric layers to prevent bleach from bleeding through to other side.

3. Pluck several petals from flowers to insure shape will be captured in print.

6. Lightly spray bleach around edges of each flower.

7. Allow bleach to set until color starts to change (approximately one minute).

8. Remove flowers from pillowcase.

9. When desired color is achieved, thoroughly rinse pillowcase in bucket of water.

10. Run pillowcase through washing machine and dryer.

Tips:

- Children should be supervised by an adult while completing project.

- When spraying bleach, be certain not to oversaturate fabric.

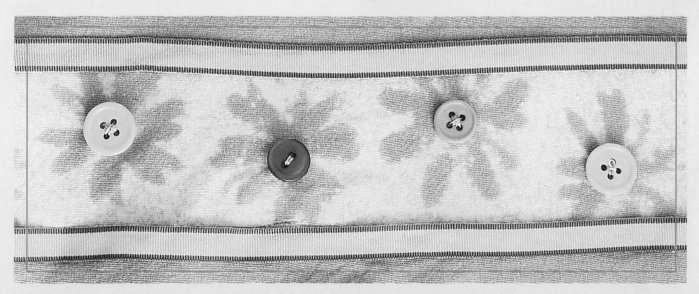

Idea: *This border design was finished on both sides with a narrow strip of ribbon. Buttons were added to the flower centers for a playful look.*

Summer
projects

Veggie-printed Apron

Kabi Cook

Materials:

acrylic paints

apron

cloth

cutting board

iron and ironing board

kitchen knife

mild laundry detergent

newspaper

selected vegetables

small paintbrushes

textile medium

Note: We used mushrooms, tomatoes, and green peppers. This technique is also adaptable for fruit such as star fruit, pomegranates, oranges, peaches, or apples.

Process:

1. Wash and dry apron. Iron if necessary.

2. Place apron on flat work surface.

3. Using knife and cutting board, slice vegetables in half. *Note: Thin slices are more difficult to hold.*

4. Using paintbrush, mix two parts paint with one part textile medium on newspaper.

5. Lightly paint cut portion of vegetable.

6. Press vegetable firmly to fabric for 10–20 seconds without wiggling or moving it.

7. Lift vegetable straight off fabric.

8. Repeat for different shapes and colors in the desired pattern. If you are overlapping the prints, let one layer dry before adding another layer.

9. Let air-dry at room temperature.

Heat-setting Paint:

1. Set iron at appropriate heat for fabric.

2. Lay apron painted side down, on cloth-covered ironing board.

3. Place another cloth over painted area and press for 20 seconds, making certain not to wiggle iron.

4. Repeat as needed over entire painted area.

5. Wash and dry apron.

Tips:

- Mix paints on newspaper for easy, recyclable cleanup.

- Try outlining vegetable/fruit veins, seeds, or edges with a thin paintbrush for a clip-art appearance.

- Practice painting produce and pressing onto scrap paper until desired results are achieved.

- Produce prints may be used as a border, as an allover, random pattern, or alone as a focal point of apron or other fabric project.

Gyotaku T-shirt

Marni G. Lee

Materials:

- cardboard squares
- cotton T-shirt
- fabric paints
- iron and ironing board
- large table
- newspaper
- paintbrushes of all sizes
- plate
- paper towels
- partially thawed frozen fish
- pins with very small heads
- plastic cup

Process:

1. Cover table and floor with newspaper to protect from spills.

2. Lay fish on newspaper with cardboard under fins. Pin fins open.

3. Place desired amount of paint on plate, limiting colors to three.

4. Using a different brush for each color, brush light coat of paint over entire fish in direction of scales, working quickly before paint dries.

5. Remove pins and place fish on clean newspaper to minimize mess. Spread fins open.

6. Rub shirt gently over entire fish, including fins, without letting shirt wiggle.

7. Remove shirt by lifting slowly. Let shirt dry on newspaper overnight.

Tip: Practice on paper to perfect the design before printing on cloth.

Heat-setting paint:

1. Set iron at appropriate heat for fabric.

2. Lay T-shirt painted side down.

3. Place cloth over painted area and press for 20 seconds.

4. Repeat as needed over entire painted area.

5. Machine-wash using mild soap and a gentle wash cycle, then air-dry.

Tips:

- Wear old clothes in case any paint spills.

- Have a friend help when you print to support underside of fins and help with placement of print.

- If there is too much paint on fish, dab with a paper towel, or print it on scrap paper to remove some paint, do touch-ups, then print on fabric.

designed by Marg Hjelmstad

Tip: Make fish print on watercolor paper, using a solid color. When dry, brush with watercolors over image to create "water."

Fish-stamped Print

Fred B. Mullett

Materials:

black ink

fish pattern rubber stamp

gum-backed mailing tape

spray bottle

stamp cleaner

stamp positioner with clear acrylic plate

water-based markers

white water-based paint

watercolor brush, small #1 or #2

watercolor paper

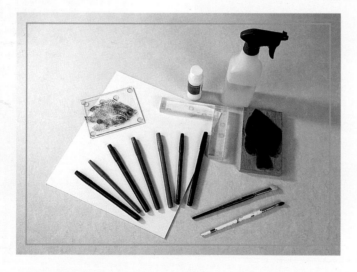

Process:

1. Tape edges of paper to work surface to insure a smooth surface and prevent warping. Soak watercolor paper with water. Stretch and smooth paper. Let dry completely.

2. Apply water-based marker to rubber stamp.

3. Spray stamp with fine mist of water. *Note: The amount of water you spray should appear excessive as you are trying to break down the detail and fill in the shape with color.*

4. Stamp image near the lower center of the page. *Note: This is the image on which you will be adding detail later.*

5. Spray stamp again and repeat, tilting images up and down to suggest movement, and overlapping to suggest depth. *Note: Do not add more color to stamp during this process.* Let dry completely.

6. Cover stamp with black ink and press onto clear acrylic plate, lining up stamp in top right corner.

7. Place plate over first stamped image, lining up image exactly.

8. Place stamp positioner so that it lines up along the top and side edge of the plate.

9. Remove plate, leaving positioner in place.

10. Clean black ink from stamp.

11. Selectively apply some darker and more vibrant marker colors to portions of stamp and fade them away. *Note: Shape the white of the eye using a darker color on the bottom to suggest shadow and then fade up.*

12. Spray with a fine mist of water. Stamp over first stamped image, lining up corner of stamp into corner of stamp positioner. Let dry completely.

13. Repeat Steps 11 and 12, layering up with darker and more intense colors to make the image more exciting. Experiment with different colors and shapes to create unique patterns.

14. Add black dot in the center of eye for iris. With white paint, add a small white highlight to eye.

15. Let artwork dry for several days.

Tip:

- Practice on a scrap sheet of watercolor paper until you achieve the desired results.

Idea: *If you would like to continue experimenting with fish prints, there are many rubber stamp images available to further your creativity. The paint or stamp technique will drastically change the look.*

The examples shown below and right were designed by Suze Weinberg. For more detail on these stamping techniques, her book, The Art of Rubber Stamping, *is a great resource. The rubber stamps used are from* Fred B. Mullet's Stamps from Nature *collection.*

Two layers of embossing enamel were used on the background paper below to create a cracked, aged look. The background was then lightly wiped with brown ink, which seeped into the cracks. When dry, the fish images were stamped in black.

designed by Suze Weinberg

For the background shown above, adhere fusible webbing to cardstock and melt embossing powders over the top. As the powders melt, they create holes in the webbing. Then stamp fish in black on white paper, color with markers, cut out and transfer.

To create the mottled look at right, roll water-based ink with a brayer onto glossy cardstock. While still wet, sprinkle with salt. Once salt has dried, brush off excess. The design was stamped in black for a more dramatic look.

Foil Art
Wes Groesbeck

Materials:

craft knife

heavy-aluminum foil

leaves, pine needles,
    dried flowers, etc.

mat board

paper tape

ruler

spray mount adhesive

wax shoe polish

pencil

picture frame

rag

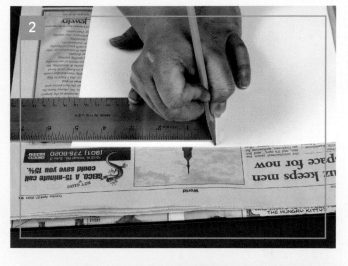

Process:

1. Take a walk in nature to collect interesting
    objects to make a textural wall piece. *Note:
    Dry items work best since they will not
    decay.*

2. Using ruler, pencil, and craft knife,
    measure and cut mat board to fit frame.

3. Lightly apply spray adhesive to mat board.

4. Arrange objects on mat board to create desired texture.

5. Cover objects with aluminum foil.

6. Press foil firmly over surface.

7. Tape foil to back of mat board.

8. Finger-press foil around object to create a raised surface.

9. If desired, use rag to apply shoe polish to heighten texture. Let dry for approximately 20 minutes, then frame.

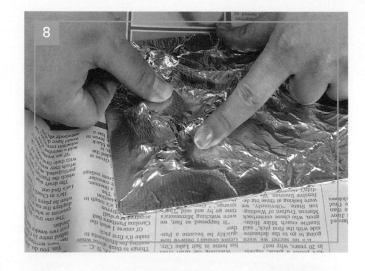

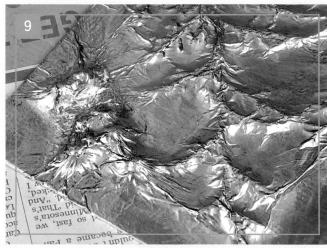

Etched Glassware

Mary McKinley

Materials:

- eye protection
- glass-etching cream
- rubber gloves
- scissors
- set of wine glasses and glass plates
- small leaves from plants such as ivy, china doll, or bamboo: one leaf for each glass, and three leaves for each plate
- small paintbrush

Note: Not suitable for children. Etching cream can be quite hazardous. Be certain to follow manufacturer's instructions, use in a well-ventilated area, use rubber gloves, and wear long sleeves and eye protection.

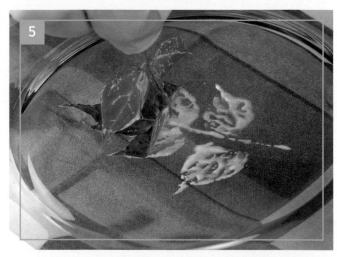

Process:

1. Thoroughly wash and dry wine glasses and glass plates.

2. Cut small leaves from plants, and make certain they are dry.

3. Wearing rubber gloves and eye protection and using paintbrush, coat back side of leaf thickly with etching cream, following manufacturer's instructions.

4. Using end of paintbrush, carefully press entire leaf onto outside of glass surface.

5. Carefully peel leaf from glass. Let dry, following manufacturer's instructions.

6. Wash glass thoroughly.

Cement Bird Feeder

Ruth Knight

Materials:

20 pounds quick-setting cement

cardboard box, at least 20" x 18" x 6"

color additive (optional, if colored cement is desired)

cement sealer

fine sand, enough to fill 2 five gallon buckets

heavy plastic sheet or heavy-duty garbage bag

large leaves from plants such as catalpa tree, hosta, dock, rhubarb, or squash

mixing stick

textile paint (optional, if a painted bird feeder is desired)

paintbrush

rubber gloves

hand shovel or trowel

toothbrush

utility knife

Process:

1. Line cardboard box with heavy plastic. Mound sand in box at least 2"–3" thick, then wet thoroughly. Cover mound with plastic.

2. Dampen leaf so it is soft and pliable, then place leaf veiny side up on plastic.

3. Wearing rubber gloves and using mixing stick, mix cement until consistency of cake batter, following manufacturer's instructions. Add color additive if desired.

4. Cover leaf with at least ½" of cement mixture, and spread to smooth. Spray with water to moisten.

5. Using knife, trim edge of wet cement, neatly tracing edge of leaf.

6. Cover cement with plastic and let dry. *Note: Drying can take 24 hours or more.*

7. Turn right side up and peel off leaf, using toothbrush or knife to rid cement of any remaining pieces.

8. Apply paint if painted bird feeder is desired. Allow to dry thoroughly.

9 Using paintbrush, apply cement sealer to bird feeder. Let dry.

Idea: *To make a birdbath using this same technique, mound sand higher to create more depth in your mold so that the curve of the cement will be deep enough to hold water.*

YIELD
4 servings

TOTAL TIME
About 1½ hours
plus cooling time

NUTRITIONAL
ANALYSIS
PER SERVING
Calories 216
Protein 1 g
Carbohydrates 43 g
Fat 5 g
Saturated fat 2 g
Cholesterol 12 mg
Sodium 1 mg

The succes

For th is reca

more than ar

then is dilute

4   Anjou or B
    (about 2 po

2   teaspoons un

1   tablespoon le

¼   cup sugar

3   tablespoons M
    Mint leaves, fo

1. Preheat the oven

2. Do not remove th
but peel them with
using a melon baller,
teaspoon measuring s
from the base.

3. Melt the butter in
Stir in the lemon juice.
mixture, and sprinkle th

146

Decorative Fruit Tile

Suzy Skadburg

Materials:

kitchen knife

paintbrush

paint pen

paper plate

paper towel

porcelain paints

pears, apples, bananas, or other firm fruit

tile

Process:

1. Pour three different colors of paint onto paper plate.

2. Using paintbrush, mix paints with water.

3. Cut fruit in half.

4. Paint the cut surface of fruit with all three colors until completely covered.

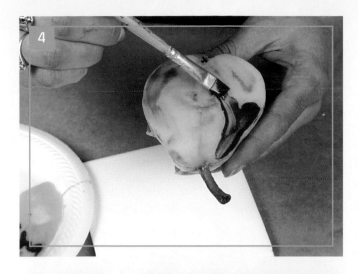

5. Test your print by pressing on a paper towel. If there are bare spots in print, add more paint to fruit.

6. Press fruit firmly down on tile.

7. Lift up carefully. If there are bare spots, use paintbrush to fill in.

8. Drop a few drops of water over paint on tile for a watercolored look.

9. Let dry for several hours.

10. Use paint pen to draw in details such as stem, leaves, and seeds.

11. Let dry thoroughly, for approximately 24 hours.

12. Bake tile in oven according to paint manufacturer's instructions.

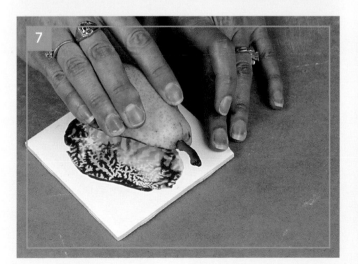

Idea: *Use a larger size tile to create pretty pot holders. Place adhesive felt squares under the tile so that it doesn't scratch the countertop. This would be a fun gift for children to make for family and neighbors.*

Autumn
projects

Project 14

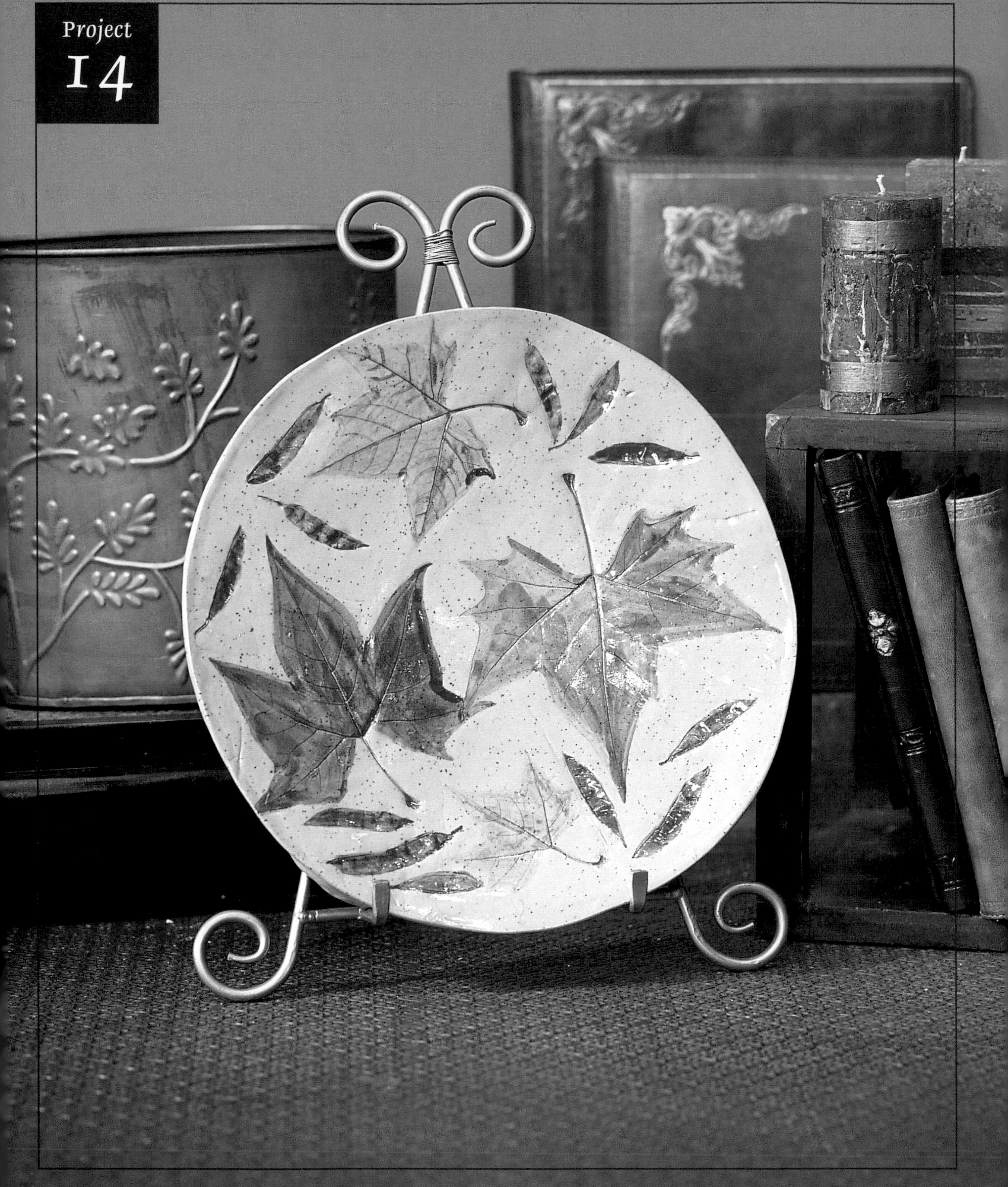

Decorative Serving Platter

Wes Groesbeck

Make Hump Mold

Materials:

2 wooden dowels, ¾" in diameter and 6" long

10 pounds plaster

13" diameter metal wastebasket

canvas, at least 15" sq.

craft knife

five-gallon mixing bucket

nylon scouring pad

15" of rope

stirring stick

Process:

1. Pull canvas tautly over rim of wastebasket and secure with rope below rim. Place one 6" wooden dowel between rope and canvas on each side of wastebasket and twist like a tourniquet to pull canvas tight.

2. Using bucket and stirring stick, mix plaster, following manufacturer's instructions.

3. Pour plaster into center of canvas slowly and carefully to prevent air bubbles from forming.

4. Firmly tap sides of wastebasket to dislodge any bubbles in plaster. Let dry for one hour.

5. Remove plaster hump mold from canvas and smooth out any irregularities with craft knife and/or nylon scouring pad.

6. Set hump mold aside where air can circulate around it freely. Let mold dry out thoroughly before using. *Note: Never rush drying time by placing mold in oven or kiln; if plaster gets too hot it will break down and mold will not work.*

Make Decorative Platter

Materials:

2½"-diameter sponge

4¼" potter's finishing rubber

3½ pounds cone-five clay

assorted plant material, soaked overnight in water

banding wheel or lazy susan

craft knife

electric or gas-fired kiln

newspaper

nylon scouring pad

low- or high-fire overglaze

medium and large plastic bags

rolling pin or slab roller

ruler

scale

scissors

underglaze

wooden pottery bat

wooden skewer or sharp pencil

Process:

1. Using rolling pin, roll clay to approximately ¼" thick and at least 15" in diameter.

2. Place clay on large wooden bat covered with newspaper. Cut piece of paper to diameter of hump mold and center it on top of clay as a pattern.

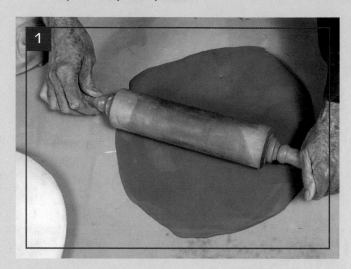

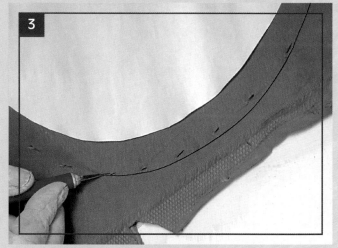

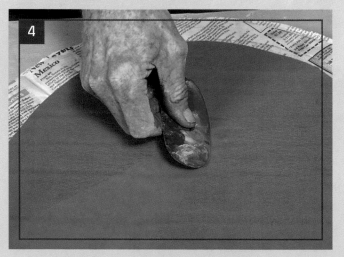

3. Using wooden skewer, trace a circle approximately 1" outside pattern. Using craft knife, cut away excess clay and store in medium-sized bag.

4. Remove pattern from clay. Using potter's finishing rubber, smooth out clay.

5. Place pattern again on center of platter and softly outline to provide border for decoration. Remove pattern.

6. Using sponge, gently press plant material into platter in desired pattern within border markings.

7. Remove border markings with sponge and place pattern back onto platter.

8. Using craft knife and pattern, trim away excess clay from platter's rim. Do not remove pattern.

9. Smooth edge of rim with sponge and potter's finishing rubber.

10. Place convex side of hump mold on clay in center of paper.

11. With one hand on top of flat side of hump mold and one hand under bat, quickly flip hump mold so that clay is now covering convex portion of mold.

12. Place flat portion of hump mold on banding wheel. Remove bat and newspaper from hump mold.

13. Press dried plant material into bottom of platter to decorate as desired.

Dry and Finish Platter:

1. Enclose entire platter and hump mold in large plastic bag for 12 hours. *Note: This will allow moisture in clay to equalize.*

2. Remove plastic bag and let platter dry on mold for two hours, until clay is hard.

3. Remove platter from mold, invert, and place in newspaper tent. *Note: This will allow platter to dry slowly and prevent cracking.* Let dry thoroughly.

4. Using craft knife and scouring pad, trim and smooth any rough or irregular areas. *Note: There is no need to remove plant material embedded in clay as it will burn out during bisque-firing.*

Bisque-fire and Glaze Platter:

1. Bisque-fire platter in kiln to cone five or 1891°F, when platter is bone dry.

2. After bisque-firing, underglazes can be used to further decorate platter.

3. Either low- or high-fire glaze can be applied to finish platter, following manufacturer's instructions.

Idea: *This charming geranium leaf pot was made by combining six clay leaves. A small ball of clay was flattened and used as the base. Make certain to score all edges where they come in contact with the base or adjoining leaf.*

designed by Susan Alexander and Taffnie Bogart

Homemade Greeting Cards

Kabi Cook

Materials:

- assorted acrylic paints
- good-quality cardstock or stationery
- newspaper
- paintbrushes
- paper plate
- scissors
- scratch paper (optional)
- sturdy, flat leaves, flowers, or other natural materials

4. Apply paint to entire surface of leaf. Use a very thin layer of paint to reveal the maximum detail of the leaf.

5. Remove leaf from newspaper and gently press painted side onto card, being careful to press along the stem and around the edges to get the full print of the leaf onto the paper.

Process:

1. Carefully cut and/or fold paper into desired shape. *Note: Try cutting the card into a leaf shape or other design.*

2. Squeeze small amount of paint onto paper plate.

3. Place leaf onto newspaper with veiny, defined side up.

6. Carefully lift leaf from paper.

7. Repeat with different shapes and colors for creative pattern. *Note: If you are layering your prints, let each one dry before layering a new one on top.*

8. Let air-dry for one hour.

9. If desired, embellish your cards with a creative border.

Tips:

- An alternate technique is to coat a thin layer of paint on a piece of scratch paper and press leaf into paint, then lift up leaf and press onto card.

- Fragile plants and flowers can only be printed once or twice and may require practice with scrap paper before printing on a card. Sturdier leaves and plants can be reprinted as many as 20 times.

designed by Suze Weinberg

*dear jennifer
thanks for
the really
lovely gift!

Mom*

designed by Suze Weinberg

Idea: *Try using gold paint or rolling on "rainbow ink" using a colored stamp pad and brayer.*

67

Thank You

Watercolor Notecards

Suzy Skadburg

Materials:

flowers, leaves, or other natural material

good-quality cardstock or stationery

mild liquid soap

paintbrushes

paper bag, newspaper, or other flat painting
   surface

paper plate

paper towels

practice paper

scissors

tweezers

watercolor paints

3. Place leaf rightside down on paper bag and
   brush on very thin coating of soap mixture
   to help paint adhere to plant.

4. Immediately brush leaf and stem with paint
   mixture.

5. Lift leaf by stem and place it paint side
   down on card, taking care not to wiggle
   leaf. *Note: You may wish to use tweezers to
   prevent paint from rubbing off stem.*

Process:

1. Using paintbrush, mix paint with equal
   amount of water on paper plate until
   consistency of cream.

2. On another paper plate, mix ½ teaspoon
   liquid soap with 1 tablespoon water.

6. Cover leaf with paper towel and press gently with hands.

7. Slowly remove paper towel. Using tweezers, remove leaf from print. Let dry.

Tips:

- Use spray bottle to evenly moisten a large leaf just before printing.

- Leaves can be repainted and reused.

- Keep watercolor covered with plastic wrap when not in use to keep from drying out. If water colors do dry out, add a few drops of water, wait a few minutes, and mix.

- Try watercoloring over an inked print.

- Experiment with two or three colors, blending them on the plant with a brush before printing.

- Save smeared or blurred prints by reprinting over them with brighter or darker colors. The blurriness of the first print will make them appear to be in the background, and the sharp colors of the second print will make them seem to be in the foreground.

- Try using using a watercolor wash on finished, dry prints to add more depth and color.

designed by Suze Weinberg

Idea: Ink pads can help create a watercolored look. Try stamping leaves and flowers with archival ink in a lighter color on glossy cardstock, then brayering in rainbow ink when dry.

Feather Cyanoprint
Suzy Skadburg

Materials:

cyanotype blueprinting square for fabric

black tea (optional)

bucket of water

foam board or empty box

feathers

newspaper (optional)

salt (optional)

T-pins

Process:

1. Place blueprinting square on foam board.

2. Place feathers on blueprinting square in desired design and pin in place.

3. Place square in direct sunlight for 10 minutes on warm, sunny days; 15 minutes on cool, sunny days; or 20 minutes on cold, sunny days.

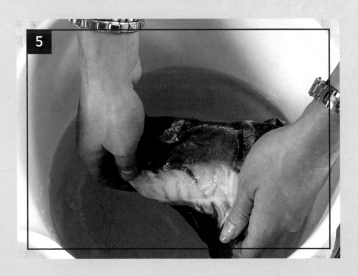

4. Remove feathers and take indoors or in deep shade to rinse.

5. Rinse cloth in bucket of water, changing water 3–4 times, until water is clear. Be certain to avoid sunlight while rinsing.

6. Dry in a clothes dryer, or air-dry on a stack of newspaper away from direct sunlight.

Tips:

- If newspaper begins to show traces of blue while drying, the print is not thoroughly rinsed and should be returned to water.

- To retain the blue color, cyanoprints should be laundered only with liquid hand or laundry soap, as soaps that contain phosphates or washing sodas will cause the blue color to fade and turn yellow.

- To create a brown print, soak cyano-print in solution of one gallon hot water and one tablespoon of salt per yard of fabric until cloth turns yellow. Then rinse, dry, and soak cloth in black tea until yellow areas turn brown and white areas are slightly tinted. Then rinse and dry again.

Project 18

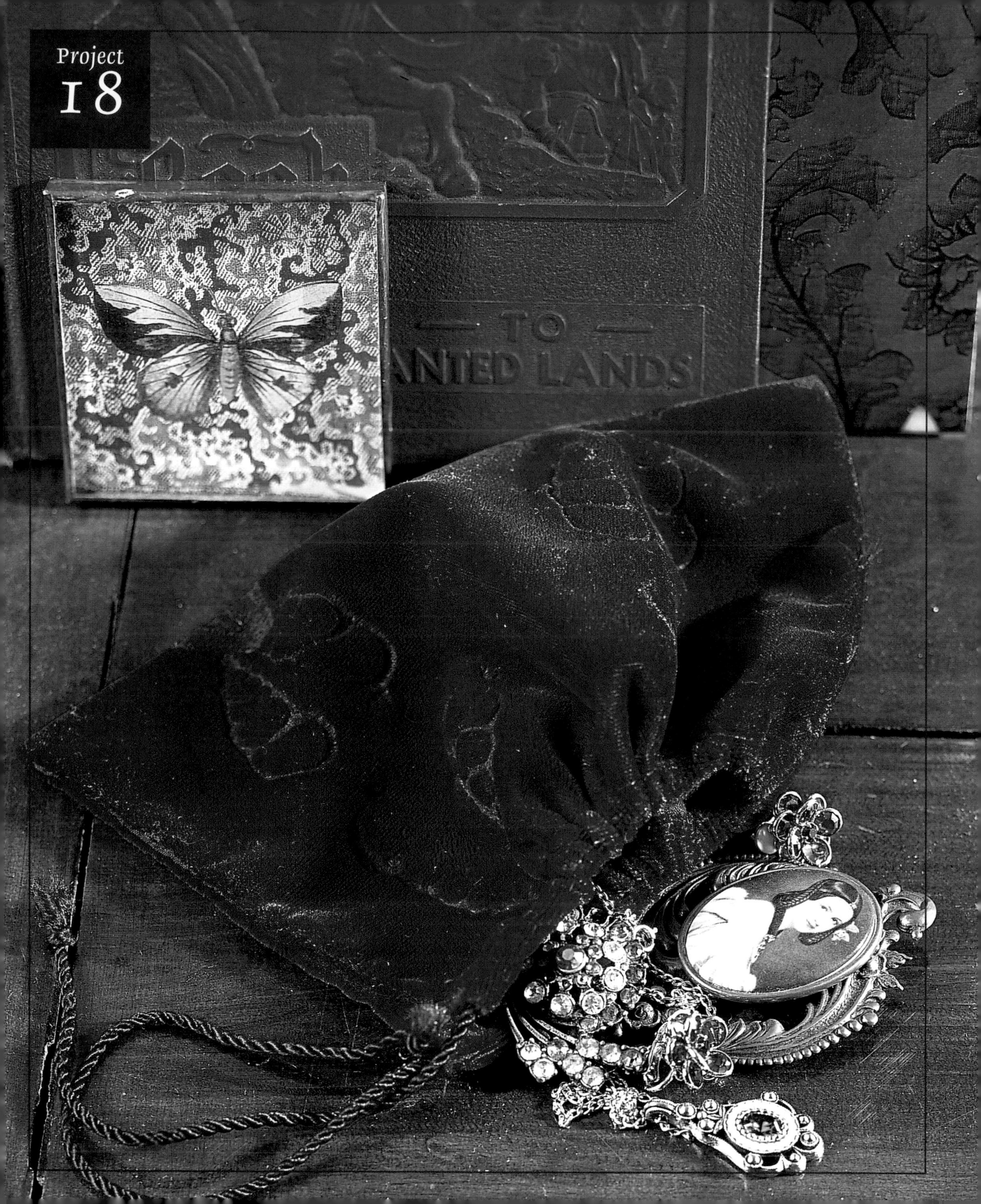

Burnt-velvet Pouch

Mary Jane Catlin and Dorothy Johnson

Materials:

acrylic velvet, 12" x 9"

decorative cord

iron and ironing board

ruler

safety pin

scissors

sewing machine

sliced shells

spray bottle

sturdy foam

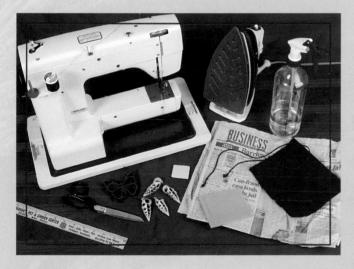

Process:

1. Heat iron to medium high.

2. Place shells on foam in desired design, then place velvet, nap side down, onto shells.

3. Spray liberally with water and press firmly with iron for 20–25 seconds, taking care not to wiggle iron.

Sewing:

1. Sew with narrow zigzag stitch along 9" edge, then fold stitched edges in ¾" and zigzag-stitch along inside edge for cord header.

2. Fold fabric in half, right sides together, with header at top. Using ¼" seam allowance, zigzag-stitch along sides, up to header.

3. Thread cord through header with safety pin. Knot ends of cord.

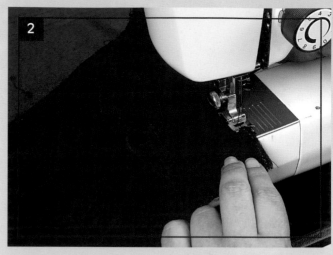

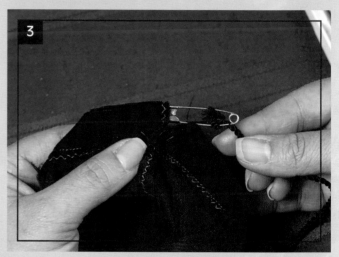

Idea: *A rubber stamp can also be used to create the burnt-velvet look. Be certain to use a flat-back stamp without a handle so that it lays flush on the surface.*

designed by Personal Stamp Exchange

Leaf-printed Scarf
Roberta Glidden

Materials:

- 15" x 72" silk charmeuse scarf
- brayer
- gutta resist, with applicator
- iron and ironing board
- leaves with definite vein patterns
- metallic fabric paint
- newspaper
- paintbrushes
- phone book or newspaper
- plastic cups
- press cloth
- silk dyes
- sponge brush
- straight pins
- wooden cork-lined scarf frame

Process:

1. Place leaf on phone book. Brush metallic fabric paint on back of leaf.

2. Place scarf right side up on newspaper.

3. Position leaf upside down on scarf and burnish with brayer. Repeat to create random pattern.

4. Let leaves dry, then remove.

Heat-setting Paint:

1. Set iron at appropriate heat for silk.

2. Lay scarf, painted side down, on cloth covered ironing board.

3. Place cloth over painted area and cover with pressing cloth. Press for 20 seconds. Repeat as needed over entire painted area.

Dyeing Scarf:

1. Pin scarf to frame. Mist with water to stretch silk if necessary.

2. Pour desired color dye into plastic cup. Dip sponge brush into dye. Smoothly drag brush across scarf until completely covered. Let dry thoroughly, according to dye manufacturer's instructions.

Outlining Pattern:

1. Outline leaf shapes on scarf with gutta resist. Make certain it penetrates through fabric. Let dry. *Note: Gutta resist is used to draw borders of an image on silk, stopping the flow of dye at resist lines.*

2. Fill in leaf shapes on scarf with dye of contrasting colors. Let dry thoroughly, according to dye manufacturer's instructions.

Steaming

Note: All silk fabric painted with silk dye must be steamed to set the color.

Materials:

large canner with rack and lid

newsprint paper

plate

dish soap

heavy pan or other weight

heavy-duty aluminum foil

tape

towel

Process:

1. Roll scarf in newsprint paper and tape bundle securely.

2. Pour 1" water into canner with metal rack inside. Place on stove over low heat.

3. Place silk bundle in canner on plate, with plenty of space between sides and top.

4. Create an "umbrella" with foil over silk bundle to prevent condensation from wetting silk. Do not wrap foil tightly.

5. Place folded towel between top of canner and lid to absorb steam. Make certain corners of towel are well above stovetop.

6. Place inverted heavy pan on lid to retain steam.

7. Steam silk for approximately one hour, following dye manufacturer's instructions.

8. Remove silk from canner and unroll bundle. Hang silk to dry for approximately 12 hours, then rinse and let dry thoroughly.

9. Remove gutta resist, following manufacturer's instructions.

Idea: *Try using prints from several kinds of leaves, and experimenting with different colors.*

designed by Roberta Glidden

Winter
projects

the pleasure of your company
is requested at the marriage of

heidi sackinsky
and
lance koudele

friday, the twenty-eighth of september
two thousand and one
five o'clock
cove vineyards
oregon

Nature Paper

Linda Weiskopf

Materials:

- blender
- books or a paper/flower press
- felt or pellon (fabric liner available at fabric stores) cut to be approximately 1"–2" larger than papermaking screens on all sides
- natural materials such as dried flower petals, dried and fresh leaves or herbs, or pine needles
- papermaking frame/deckle
- paper shredder or scissors
- recycled papers, such as telephone books, newspaper, copier paper, craft scraps, etc.
- utility sponge
- waterproof container at least 3" deep and at least 2" larger than papermaking screens. (We used a litter box and a plastic storage container.)
- white or colored tissue paper (optional)

Notes: Makes 1–15 pieces, depending on size of container. We used a paper shredder, which is quickest, but children may enjoy tearing or using safe scissors.

Process:

1. Shred, tear, or cut papers into small strips or scraps, keeping colors separate.

2. Select desired color and place three handfuls of shredded paper into blender.

3. Add warm water until blender is approximately ½ full. Pulse on high until thoroughly pulverized. *Note: For a chopped up look, add a handful of natural material.*

5. Place felt on flat, dry surface.

6. Fill waterproof container approximately half full with warm water.

7. Add blended pulp to water. *Note: For a 14" x 19" x 6" container, add approximately nine cups (three average-sized blender batches). For 11" x 14" x 3" container, add approximately 6 cups (2 average-sized blender batches).*

8. Stir pulp mixture in container with your hand until uniform in texture.

9. If desired, sprinkle a small handful of natural materials into the container of pulp and water. Materials will probably float.

10. Assemble frame, screen on bottom, and press straight down into pulp mixture.

11. Shake gently just under surface of water until desired amount of natural material is visible on top of frame.

12. Gently lift straight up, keeping frame over container.

13. Let water drip from frame, shaking gently to hasten process.

14. While still holding frame over container, blot excess water on screen with sponge, squeezing out sponge when necessary.

15. When drip has stopped, place one hand on top of frame furthest from your body and lift deckle toward you, separating it from the screen. Set deckle aside.

16. Holding screen over container, blot off water on sides and bottom.

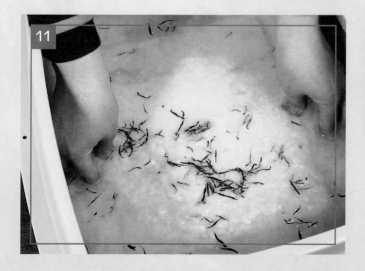

17. Flip screen upside down onto felt.

18. Press sponge on screen to soak up excess water. Repeat until screen and pulp are as dry as possible.

19. Lift screen straight up off pulp in one motion. *Note: If desired, add more natural materials here on top of pulp.*

20. Let pulp (now your paper) partially dry about 5–12 hours, depending on thickness of paper.

21. *Note: For double-sided paper, cover entire paper with very thin tissue paper. Using sponge, gently moisten all the tissue paper, taking care not to introduce wrinkles to the paper, tissue, or natural materials. If desired, add additional plant materials for more texture. Follow through with drying process.*

22. When partially dry, press paper with books. Alternate between pressing and air-drying, as paper will be very difficult to get flat if it dries completely without any pressing.

Tips:

- If paper comes out too thick or thin, just throw it back into vat of water and pulp.

- Too much pulp in the container will make very thick paper. Too little will make paper too thin. Experiment.

- To add color to white paper, try adding one handful of shredded colored tissue paper to two handfuls of white paper.

- When sponge gets wet while blotting, squeeze water back into the pulp container.

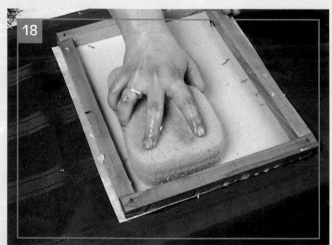

Gourd Jewelry
Linda Weiskopf

Materials:

- gourd
- keyhole saw
- paintbrush or sponge brush
- pencil
- pin backs
- pressed leaves or flowers
- sandpaper
- textile sealant
- white craft glue

Process:

1. Sand gourd.

2. Draw lines on gourd in desired shape.

3. Using tip of keyhole saw, puncture a hole in gourd along outline.

4. Cut along line, then gently release jewelry piece from gourd.

5. Sand jewelry piece, especially on edges, to insure that it will not catch on clothing.

6. Using paintbrush or sponge brush, coat leaf with sealant. After placing leaf onto jewelry piece, smooth gently and coat again with sealant.

7. Let air-dry for 20 minutes.

8. Turn piece over and glue pin onto back of piece. Let dry thoroughly.

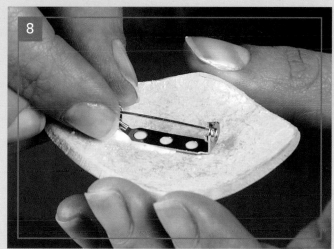

designed by Marilynn Host

designed by Marilynn Host

Idea: *Don't throw away the rest of your gourds! Instead, turn them into charming bird-houses or bird feeders. Make certain to use non-toxic paint when decorating your gourd creations.*

91

Crackers au Naturale

Mary Jane Catlin

Materials:

2 cookie sheets

basting brush

cooking spray or oil

egg whites

fillo dough

fresh herbs such as cilantro, parsley, basil, rosemary, etc.

oven

parchment paper

seasonings

wire whisk or fork

3. Spray parchment paper lightly with oil or cooking spray.

4. To the side of the cookie sheet, unfold a piece of fillo dough onto a flat surface and cut into cracker-sized shapes.

5. Place shapes on parchment paper.

6. Position herbs on dough in desired design.

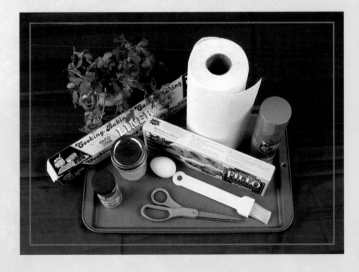

Process:

1. Using whisk, mix one egg white with equivalent amount of water in small container.

2. Spread parchment paper on cookie sheet.

7. Using basting brush, lightly spread egg-white mixture over herbs to seal dough.

8. Sprinkle seasonings onto dough.

9. Lightly spray dough with cooking spray.

10. Cover shapes with another dough layer or fold existing shapes in half.

11. Gently press to avoid air pockets.

12. Lightly spray dough again.

13. Cover with more parchment paper and lay second cookie sheet on top.

14. Bake at 400°F for approximately four minutes, until golden brown.

Tips:

- Cooking time varies depending on the weight of the cookie sheets; heavier sheets take an additional minute or so to bake.

- Edible flowers can also be used.

- The fillo dough dries out very quickly. After taking one piece to work with, roll the rest back up in package to retain moisture.

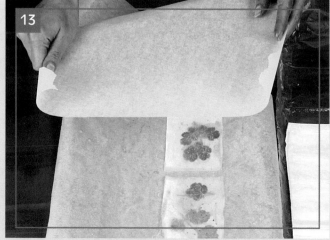

Leaf-printed Gift Wrap

Yaeko Bryner

Materials:

- 2 quarts liquid starch

- acrylic paints in desired colors

- hair rake or fork with wide tines

- leaves such as maple or oak, or paper cutouts in the shapes of leaves

- newspaper or old towel

- paper, colored or white, at least 8½" x 11" and at least 20-pound weight, such as copier paper

- shallow container such as a 10" x 13" baking pan or a plastic food storage container

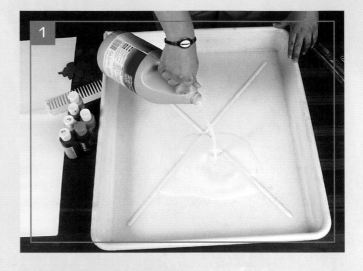

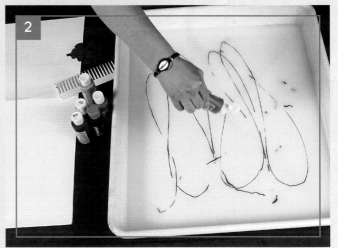

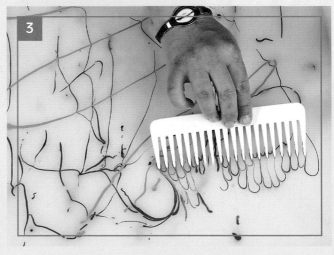

Process:

1. Pour liquid starch into container until at least 1" deep.

2. Drizzle paint onto liquid starch, using one, two, or three colors.

3. Use rake to gently swirl paint.

4. Gently place leaves on top of mixture.

5. Place a piece of paper on top of leaves, making certain paper comes into full contact with starch and paint.

6. Gently lift paper and lay flat on old towel or newspaper for 5–10 minutes until paint seems to set. Lift leaves from paper.

7. In sink, carefully rinse starch from paper.

8. Place paper flat to dry on towel or newspaper.

Tips:

- Starch and paint mixture can be reused many times.

- Try colors that match the season or holiday, such as dark green and red for Christmas; yellow, orange, and brown for Halloween, or a bright light green, yellow, or pink for spring.

- Uses for this swirled paper include:
  - Decorating a scrapbook
  - Making end papers for a handmade book or journal
  - Gluing it onto a box to create a decorative container
  - Wrapping small gifts or creating gift tags
  - Lining the inside of handmade envelopes

- While drying, the edges tend to curl. Place rocks or books on edges to weigh down.

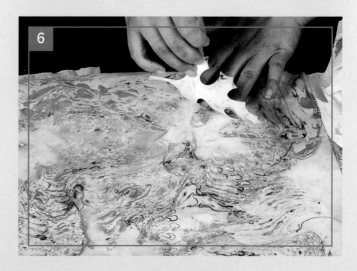

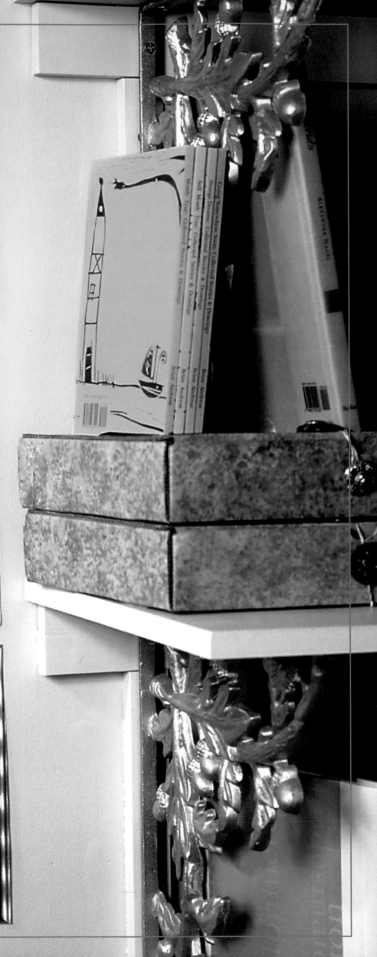

Color Copy Prints

Suzy Skadburg

Materials:

4–6 flowers with leaves, 6" tall

8 x 10" frame

8½" x 11" white paper

color copier

scissors

spray mount adhesive

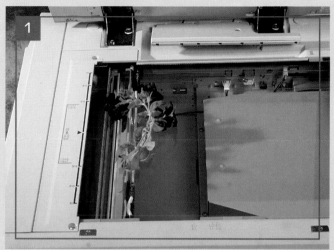

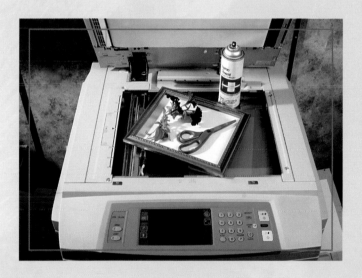

Process:

1. Arrange flowers on color copier.

2. Remove glass and back from frame and center frame over arrangement, then replace frame back.

3. Set copier at 85% and make color copy.

4. Trim edges of copy around frame.

5. Spray adhesive onto back of copy and attach to wall, where it will stay until peeled off.

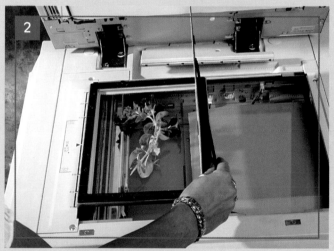

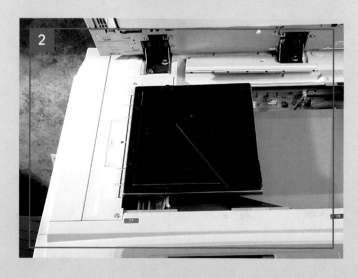

Imprinted Cookies

Karen Stayer

Make Molds

Materials:

6–8 natural items, 1½"–3⅛" tall, such as acorns, tiny pinecones, lavender sprigs, juniper sprig with berry, and small pine branches

500 grams drying clay

small, soft-bristled paintbrush

T-pin

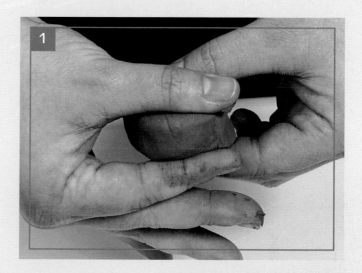

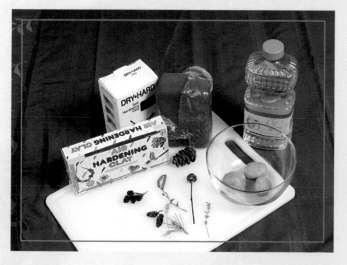

Process:

1. Knead clay until malleable and slightly warm, following manufacturer's instructions.

2. Shape clay into disk, approximately ½"–¾" thick, to create cookie mold. If desired, pinch back of mold to make small, rounded handle, approximately 2" long to make it easier to hold while pressing onto dough.

3. Center and press object firmly into front of mold, approximately ¼" deep. Lift object straight out of mold; do not wiggle. If necessary, use T-pin to lift item out or to gently remove debris. If specks are left behind, use paintbrush to remove, or blow to dislodge.

4. Let air-dry at room temperature for 24 hours or until thoroughly dry.

Tips:

- Clay may crack while pressing designs. Cracks can add to the natural design, or you can smooth them with damp finger.

- A collection of molds may be placed in a small drawstring bag as a gift.

Make Shortbread Cookies

Ingredients:

¼ cup butter at room temperature
⅓ cup powdered sugar (unsifted)
⅛ teaspoon vanilla
1 cup flour

Process:

1. Using wooden spoon, lightly cream butter in mixing bowl until completely softened.

2. Stir in powdered sugar, then vanilla. Stir until mixture is creamy. Add food coloring if desired.

3. Add enough flour to get desired firmness, kneading dough until stiff.

4. Shape dough into balls and place on cookie sheet.

5. Dip molds in white granulated sugar to prevent dough from sticking to molds, and press molds into dough balls.

6. Bake at 350°F for 10–20 minutes, until lightly browned, checking frequently.

7. Remove cookie sheet from oven and set in a cool place for approximately 10 minutes. *Note: Makes 6–8 cookies, 2"–4" wide.*

Chocolate Leaves
Suzy Skadburg

Materials:

aluminum foil
bowl
candy-making chocolate
cooking spray
fresh, sturdy, bay or other edible leaves
paintbrush
soft cloth

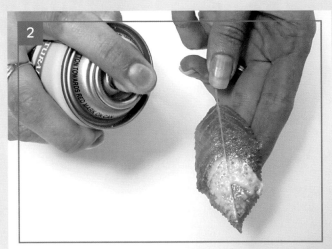

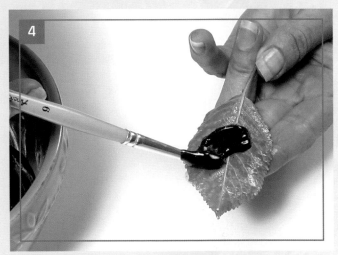

Process:

1. Spray cooking spray onto square of aluminum foil to prevent chocolate from sticking to it.

2. Clean leaves with water and dry gently with soft cloth, then apply cooking spray to prevent chocolate from sticking to leaf. Place leaves on aluminum foil.

3. Place chocolate in bowl and heat in microwave for 30 seconds, check, and continue heating just until completely melted.

4. Using paintbrush, paint leaves with chocolate, brushing from center to edges so that back of leaf remains clean.

5. Place leaves on aluminum in freezer until completely cool.

6. Dip hands in very cold water to prevent the warmth of your hands from melting the chocolate.

7. Remove chocolate covered leaves from freezer. Grasp each leaf by stem and carefully peel from chocolate.

8. Apply chocolate leaves to cake or other food item.

Tip:

- If leaf is smooth, such as an orange or bay leaf, it may be simply dragged across the surface of the melted chocolate.

Idea: *Try using white chocolate and curling the leaves before placing them in the freezer. After removing leaves, gently "paint" candy leaves with food coloring that has been diluted with water.*

designed by Jaynie Maxfield

Timeless
ideas

Natural Papers & Cards
Scrapbooks & Pages
Artwork & Collage
Gifts & Accessories

Natural Papers & Cards

designed by Rhonda Rainey

Adding vibrant colored papers to your pulp can produce dramatic results. Here, lighter pulp has been arranged amid the darker pulp, giving the illusion of beautiful roses in full bloom. Colored paper sources can include paper napkins, wrapping tissue, and construction paper. Sprinkling real rose petals into your pulp will also add beauty.

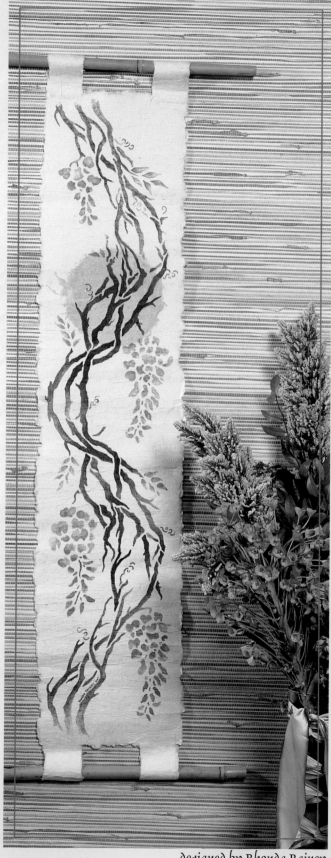

To create larger-sized paper, overlap several sheets end-to-end while they are still wet. The feathered edges will bond together when dry. This unique scroll was then printed using natural elements.

The vase below was embellished with a beautiful sheet of handmade paper and secured with gold thread. Dried decorative pulp shapes, like these metallic leaves, can be added using a liquid paper adhesive.

designed by Rhonda Rainey

designed by Rhonda Rainey

designed by Nancy Welch

designed by Rhonda Rainey

designed by Suze Weinberg

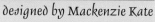

designed by Mackenzie Kate

designed by Mackenzie Kate

There are many ways that nature can be turned into art. The cards on these pages feature several techniques — leaf printing, plant pressing, even decorative stitching. Using handmade papers in your artwork also adds to the natural feel of the finished product.

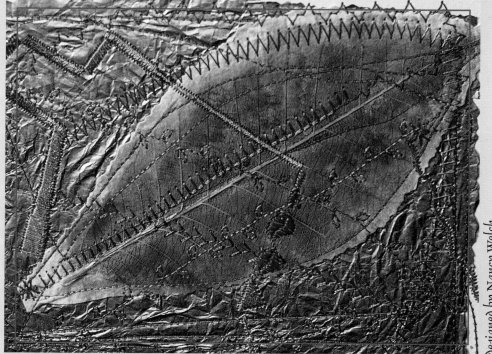

designed by Nancy Welch

111

Scrapbooks & Pages

designed by Vanessa-Ann

designed by Vanessa-Ann

designed by Vanessa-Ann

Using natural elements is a perfect choice for creating exquisite background papers for scrapbooking. The subtle nature prints combined with handmade paper especially complement vintage photographs. For a more dramatic affect, add bold touches of metallic gold. Keep your photos simple so they are not competing with the background.

designed by Vanessa-Ann

designed by Vanessa-Ann

The leaves on this scrapbook page were created by stamping leaf prints onto handmade paper. Trace leaves with a paintbrush dipped in water, and gently tear around the edges. This technique works well on any edge that you would like to "soften."

MARRIAGE OF

T M & LUCIA

For a subtle touch, layer transparent handmade paper over a fern leaf that has been mounted to a scrapbook page. Randomly attach pressed daisies across the page using spray mount.

Pressed and dried rose petals create a stunning frame for this family photo. Make certain to use several coats of decoupage medium for a lasting finish.

Artwork & Collage

This artist produces beautiful "nature quilts." Leaves, twigs, and such are hand-stitched onto textured papers all in keeping with an earthy, natural palette. The individual blocks are then hand-quilted together and beautifully framed.

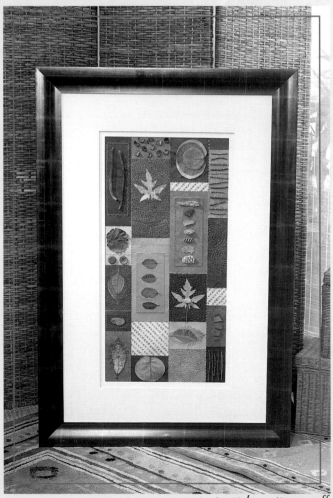

designed by Bridget Hoff

designed by Bridget Hoff

"IN MY OWN BACKYARD"

The background of this abstract collage was made by using leaves as a positive stencil, in other words, painting the outer edges. An airbrush was used to give more of an ethereal feeling; however, a paint-filled spray bottle will also produce this effect. To give her artwork dimension, the artist has added leaves and other textured materials.

designed by Susan Rothamel

designed by Rhonda Rainey

This unique vase was created using much the same technique as the Foil Art on page 46. Instead of tinfoil, tissue paper was decoupaged over bamboo pieces. Antiquing medium was then rubbed over the image to get the desired effect.

These paperweights were created by decoupaging handmade paper around smooth rocks and embellishing with threads.

The candleholders were made by decoupaging leaves on the wooden surface and highlighting with gold metallic paint.

Gold paint is also used to print a dramatic leaf design onto this dark, rich velvet. Wrapped around a candle and tied with a matching silk ribbon, this is a gift anyone would love!

designed by Rhonda Rainey

designed by Rhonda Rainey

designed by Personal Stamp Exchange

119

The Ogden Nature Center

An island of nature. That is a fitting description for the Ogden Nature Center, a 152-acre wildlife refuge in Ogden, Utah, where nature thrives and the hum of a city fades away. With a mission to unite people with nature and to nurture appreciation and stewardship of the environment, the Nature Center welcomes thousands of visitors annually.

Approximately twenty steps are all it takes to discover the peace of nature. Like landing on an island, the feeling of arrival is immediate. After turning off a busy street, visitors to the Nature Center follow a meandering path from the parking lot to the Visitor's Center, an appropriate segue, where shade trees and a whimsical neighborhood of birdhouses line the way, and meadow grass grows to the edge of the trail. Beyond this, a landscape characterized by upland fields and woodlands, riparian habitat and pathways.

People come year-round to find a place to connect with nature, whether it is hiking the trails or discovering a quiet place for a picnic. Birders come equipped with binoculars and field guides and school children arrive daily to participate in award-winning educational programs. Folks even stop by just to peruse The Nest Gift Shop with its collection of nature books, birding supplies, and educational games.

The Ogden Nature Center has the distinction of being the Intermountain West's first nature center. Founded in 1975, it began as a grassroots community effort, transforming a barren piece of land that had once been a military depot into a rich wildlife refuge and nature education center. Through the work of dedicated volunteers and staff, the Nature Center has thrived, touching the lives of almost every child in Northern Utah at some point during their elementary school careers.

From the outset, the primary focus of the Nature Center was to create a wildlife refuge. It is a varied landscape where pheasants and quail pick through fields and hawks wheel overhead. You might see a family of deer slowly foraging along in the scrub, or a group of ducks sheltering in a pond. Foxes, beaver and muskrat also live at the refuge. Migration season brings a flood of avian visitors stopping to nest. Other wild animals have come to the Nature Center in need of assistance. Every year, staff and volunteers care for hundreds of injured or orphaned wild birds. Permanently injured birds of prey such as great horned owls, bald and golden eagles, ravens, red-tailed hawks, and northern goshawks are given a second chance and have taken up residence in spacious mews adjacent to the Visitor's Center.

While the wildlife refuge is the heart of the Nature Center, its aim is really one of education, offering thousands of school children ongoing award-winning science-based programs each year. Teachers/Naturalists combine classroom learning with hands-on experiences in the field. For many, it is a first-time, up close encounter with nature. For all, it is a unique experience where the wildlife sanctuary is their classroom.

For students, a visit might mean a class about trees, which includes actually making homemade recycled paper. During winter, they may don snowshoes and trail fresh deer prints in the snow. Students study insect life, sweeping fields with nets for bugs or crawling into a mock bear den while learning about hibernation. They study aquatic organisms with microscopes, pry into owl pellets, and learn the dance of bees. Both the popular summer day camps and the year-round community programs teach students of all ages about nature and the arts, astronomy, field ecology, zoology, botany, and many other nature-related topics. Self-guided learning experiences are also available, through interpretive signs and brochures.

For this community and for the city's many visitors, Ogden Nature Center is an incredibly important asset. As an urban escape, an innovative educational facility, and a protected preserve, it is a place that constantly reminds visitors of the wonder to be found in nature. It is crucial that places such as the Nature Center are supported and sustained. Because, in the end, nature will only care for us in the same way we care for it.

— Mark R. Johnson

121

About the Contributors

Lili Bosworth has been coming to the Nature Center since she was an infant, and has been volunteering with her mother Brandi to feed the resident wild birds of prey each week. Brandi is serving as the vice chair of the Ogden Nature Center's board of directors.

Yaeko Bryner is a kindergarten teacher who, with her husband Dale, was actively involved in the formative years of the Ogden Nature Center. She is currently serving on the Nature Center's board of directors.

Mary Jane Catlin is one of the founding members of the Ogden Nature Center, and has received many awards for her volunteer work in the community. In addition to collecting rocks, leaves, and feathers, Mary Jane donates floral arrangements to her favorite nonprofit groups.

Kabi Cook is the Community Relations Coordinator at Ogden Nature Center and has been the driving force behind the creation of the projects found in this book. Kabi's passion for conservation and nature education are evident in her efforts to further the Nature Center.

Roberta Glidden is a fabric artist known for her stunning paintings on silk and nature-inspired scarves. Roberta has donated hundreds of hours to the Nature Center by teaching community education programs.

Wes Groesbeck is a skilled local potter who has taught community education programs and donated many products and time to the Ogden Nature Center. Wes is also a water-wise gardening enthusiast and raises a magnificent pumpkin patch each year.

Robert Herman is a noted architect who designed the environmentally friendly Visitor's Center at the Ogden Nature Center. A member of the board of directors, Bob has donated his talent to this and many other organizations.

Dorothy Johnson is a fabulous gardener and her friends report that everything blooms and grows for her. A retired interior decorator, Dorothy is an expert seamstress and is known for her use of unusual fabrics.

Mark Johnson is a professional freelance writer, journalist, and editor who loves the outdoors, volunteering with the U.S. Forest Service, cycling, and nature photography.

Ruth Knight is a master gardener and former board member who is retired from Weber State University. She grows unusual herbs, fruits, and heritage vegetables and flowers. She has lived all over the world.

Marni Lee is a Teacher/Naturalist at Ogden Nature Center and has taught fish printing community education classes. Her love of nature and fun teaching methods have inspired many with a desire to return to the Nature Center.

Mary McKinley is the Interim Director at Ogden Nature Center and has been actively involved as a member and a volunteer, and as Assistant Director and Director of Development. Mary credits the Nature Center with reuniting her with her love of art.

Fred B. Mullett is a member of the Nature Printing Society, and produces his own line of rubber stamps modeled after nature prints.

Suzy Skadburg is an artist who dabbles in all mediums, from watercolors to mosaics, but specializes in murals and furniture re-finishing. She is also a designer/stylist and enjoys any opportunity to create something new.

Karen Stayer is an insurance executive, serving on the Nature Center's Board of Directors. She enjoys hiking, nature photography, and creating nature-inspired needlework.

Chalae Cox Teeples is the Education Coordinator at Ogden Nature Center. She loves teaching children about the incredible things in nature. She is kept busy by caring for her family, school programs, and summer camps keep her from getting rusty during the warmer months.

Linda Weiskopf is a master gardener and avid bird-watcher who made all of her daughter's wedding invitations from homemade paper and pressed flowers. She's a busy professional who also serves on the Ogden Nature Center's Board of Directors.

Acknowledgments

Ogden Nature Center
966 West 12th Street, Ogden, UT 84404
Phone: 801-621-7595 • Fax: 801-621-1867
onc@ogdennaturecenter.org
www.ogdennaturecenter.org

p. 14
Information in "Ethics of Collecting from Nature" taken from the Washington State University Cooperative Extensions web site and from Tread Lightly.

pp. 41-44
Fred B. Mullett
Stamps from Nature Prints
P.O. Box 94502, Seattle, WA 98124 USA
Fax: 206-903-8202
Order Desk: 1-800-GYOTAKU (496-8258)
www.fredbmullett.com
rbrfish@compuserve.com

p. 72
Blue Printables
Linda Stemer - Susan McKeever
P.O. Box 2254, Vashon Island, WA 98070
1-800-356-0445 • Fax: 206-463-BLU1
info@blueprintables.com
www.blueprintables.com

Additional Project Contributors:

p. 40 . . . . Marg Hjelmstad
pp. 45, 67, 70, 110 . . . . Suze Weinberg
p. 64 . . . . Susan Alexander and Taffnie Bogart
pp. 76, 119 . . . . Personal Stamp Exchange
pp. 81, 118 . . . . Roberta Glidden
p. 91 . . . . Marilynn Host
p. 105 . . . . Jaynie Maxfield
pp. 108–110, 119. . . . . Rhonda Rainey
pp. 110–111 . . . . Nancy Welch
p. 111 . . . . Mackenzie Kate
pp. 112–115. . . . . Vanessa-Ann
p. 115. . . . . Sarah Lugg
p. 116 . . . . Bridget Hoff
p. 117. . . . . Susan Rothamel

Photodisks

p. 5 . . . . Photodisc, Inc. Images (©1993)
p. 10 . . . . Photodisc, Inc. Images (©1996)

Metric Tables

VOLUME

imperial	equivalent	metric	imperial	UK equivalent	metric
1 teaspoon [tsp.]		5 milliliter [ml]	1 fl. oz.	1.0408 UK fl. oz.	29.574 ml
3 tsp.	1 tbsp.	15 ml	1 pt.	0.8327 UK pt.	0.4731 L
2 tablespoon [tbsp.]	1 fluid ounce [fl. oz.]	30 ml	1 gal.	0.8327 UK gal.	3.7854 L
1 cup [c.]	8 fl. oz.	0.24 litre [L]			
2 c.	1 pint [pt.]	0.47 L			
4 c.	1 qt.	0.95 L			
4 quarts [qts]	1 gallon [gal.]	3.8 L			
16 tbsp.	1 c.	0.24 L			

TEMPERATURE CONVERSION EQUATIONS

degrees Fahrenheit (°F) to degrees Celsius (°C)

$$°F \text{ to } °C = (°F - 32) \times 5/9$$

$$°C \text{ to } °F = (°C \times 9/5) + 32$$

Metric Equivalency Charts

inches to millimeters [mm] and centimeters [cm]

inches	mm	cm	inches	cm	inches	cm	inches	cm
⅛	3	0.3	6	15.2	21	53.3	36	91.4
¼	6	0.6	7	17.8	22	55.9	37	94.0
⅜	10	1.0	8	20.3	23	58.4	38	96.5
½	13	1.3	9	22.9	24	61.0	39	99.1
⅝	16	1.6	10	25.4	25	63.5	40	101.6
¾	19	1.9	11	27.9	26	66.0	41	104.1
⅞	22	2.2	12	30.5	27	68.6	42	106.7
1	25	2.5	13	33.0	28	71.1	43	109.2
1¼	32	3.2	14	35.6	29	73.7	44	111.8
1½	38	3.8	15	38.1	30	76.2	45	114.3
1¾	44	4.4	16	40.6	31	78.7	46	116.8
2	51	5.1	17	43.2	32	81.3	47	119.4
3	76	7.6	18	45.7	33	83.8	48	121.9
4	102	10.2	19	48.3	34	86.4	49	124.5
5	127	12.7	20	50.8	35	88.9	50	127.0

yards to meters

meters	yards	meters	yards	meters	yards	meters	yards	meters	yards
⅛	0.11	2⅛	1.94	4⅛	3.77	6⅛	5.60	8⅛	7.43
¼	0.23	2¼	2.06	4¼	3.89	6¼	5.72	8¼	7.54
⅜	0.34	2⅜	2.17	4⅜	4.00	6⅜	5.83	8⅜	7.66
½	0.46	2½	2.29	4½	4.11	6½	5.94	8½	7.77
⅝	0.57	2⅝	2.40	4⅝	4.23	6⅝	6.06	8⅝	7.89
¾	0.69	2¾	2.51	4¾	4.34	6¾	6.17	8¾	8.00
⅞	0.80	2⅞	2.63	4⅞	4.46	6⅞	6.29	8⅞	8.12
1	0.91	3	2.74	5	4.57	7	6.40	9	8.23
1⅛	1.03	3⅛	2.86	5⅛	4.69	7⅛	6.52	9⅛	8.34
1¼	1.14	3¼	2.97	5¼	4.80	7¼	6.63	9¼	8.46
1⅜	1.26	3⅜	3.09	5⅜	4.91	7⅜	6.74	9⅜	8.57
1½	1.37	3½	3.20	5½	5.03	7½	6.86	9½	8.69
1⅝	1.49	3⅝	3.31	5⅝	5.14	7⅝	6.97	9⅝	8.80
1¾	1.60	3¾	3.43	5¾	5.26	7¾	7.09	9¾	8.92
1⅞	1.71	3⅞	3.54	5⅞	5.37	7⅞	7.20	9⅞	9.03
2	1.83	4	3.66	6	5.49	8	7.32	10	9.14

Index

tag designed by Sarah Lugg